THIS IS GONNA BE ==THE BEST YEAR OF YOUR LIFE.== WHY? BECAUSE YOU DESERVE IT. PERIOD. AND BECAUSE THIS IS THE BOOK THAT DISCOVERS WHO YOU ARE, WHAT YOU WANT AND WHAT YOU ARE DETERMINED TO ACHIEVE. LET'S GO! ==YOUR YEAR STARTS NOW!==

Name and Date:

Write what you value most about your current situation

BEING IS TO PERSEVERE IN ITS BEING

SPINOZA

WHAT'S THE MAIN CHANGE YOU NEED TO MAKE IN THE COMING MONTHS?

WHAT THINGS DO YOU HAVE THAT MANY PEOPLE WOULD LOVE TO HAVE?

Make them your priority this year!

WHAT LITTLE THINGS DO YOU VALUE THE MOST?

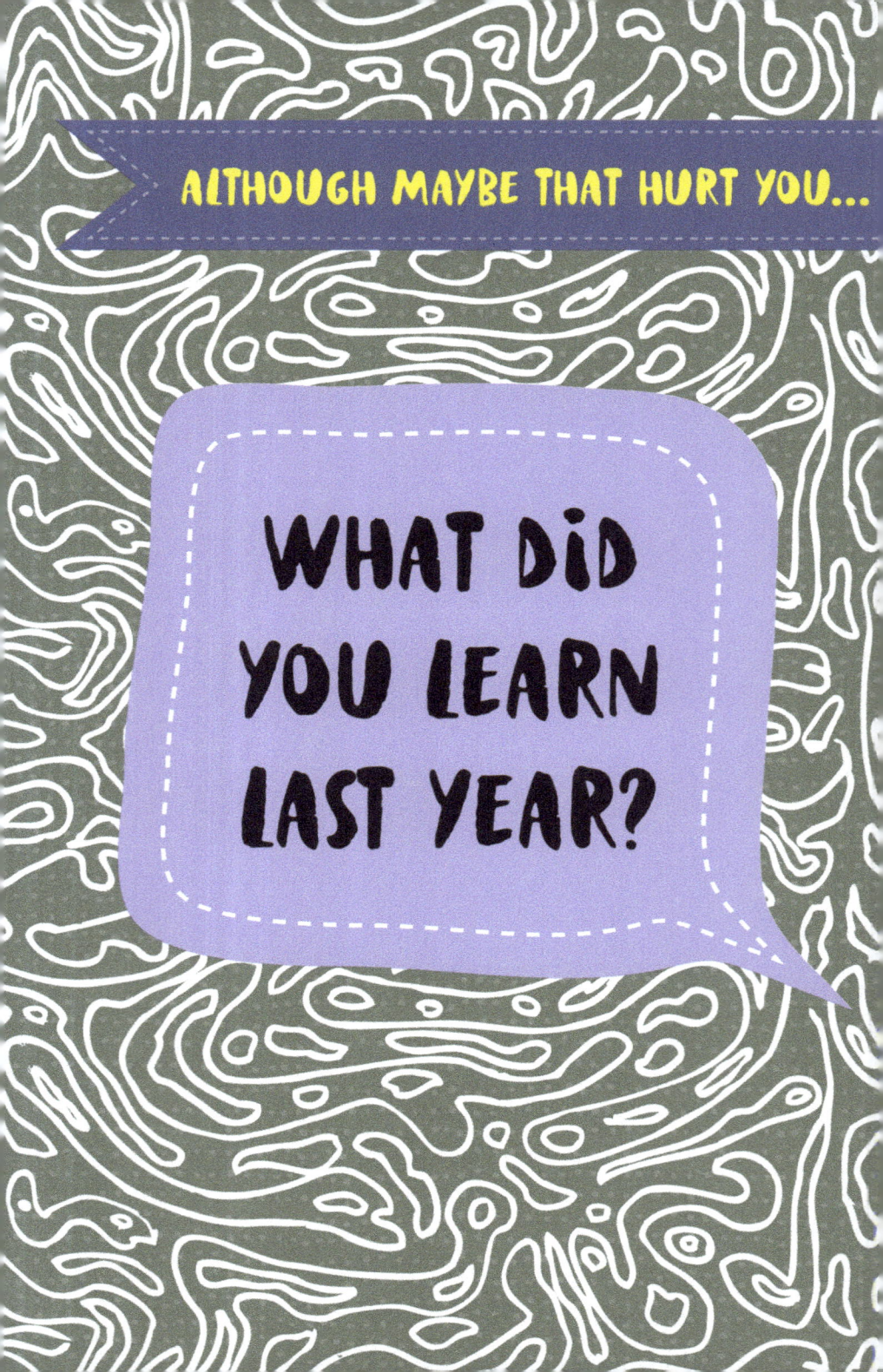

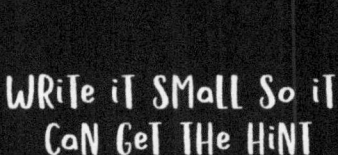

WRiTe iT SMall So iT
CaN GeT THe HiNT

WITH THE NEW DAY COMES NEW STRENGTH AND NEW THOUGHTS

"ROOSEVELT"

WHAT DO YOU NEED MOST AT THIS MOMENT?

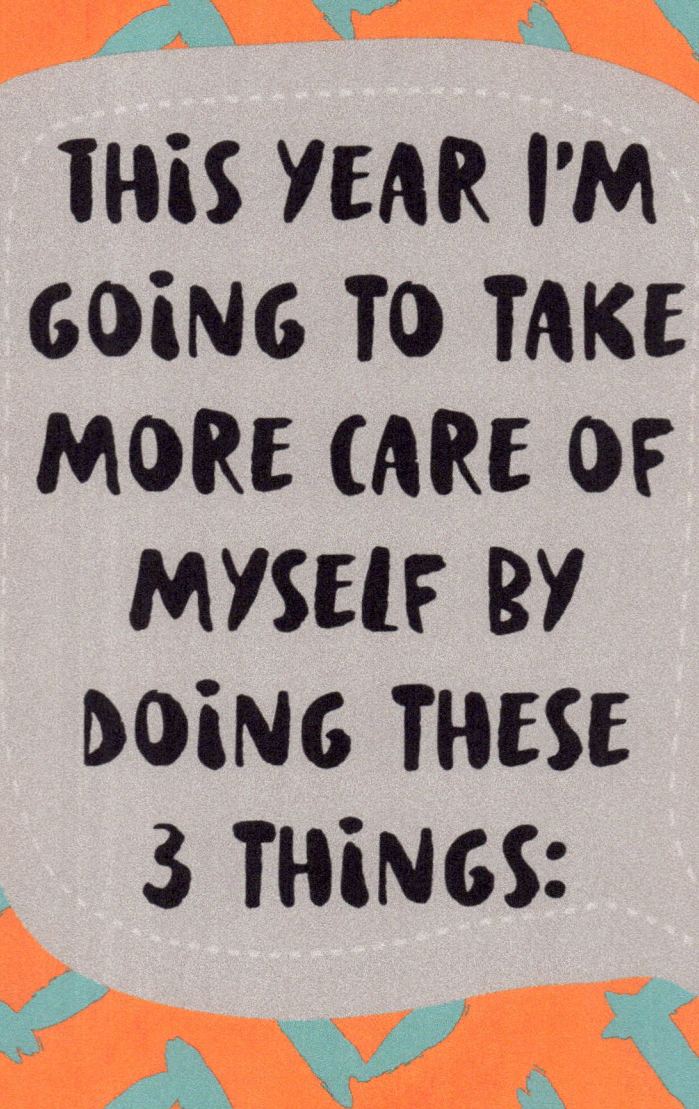

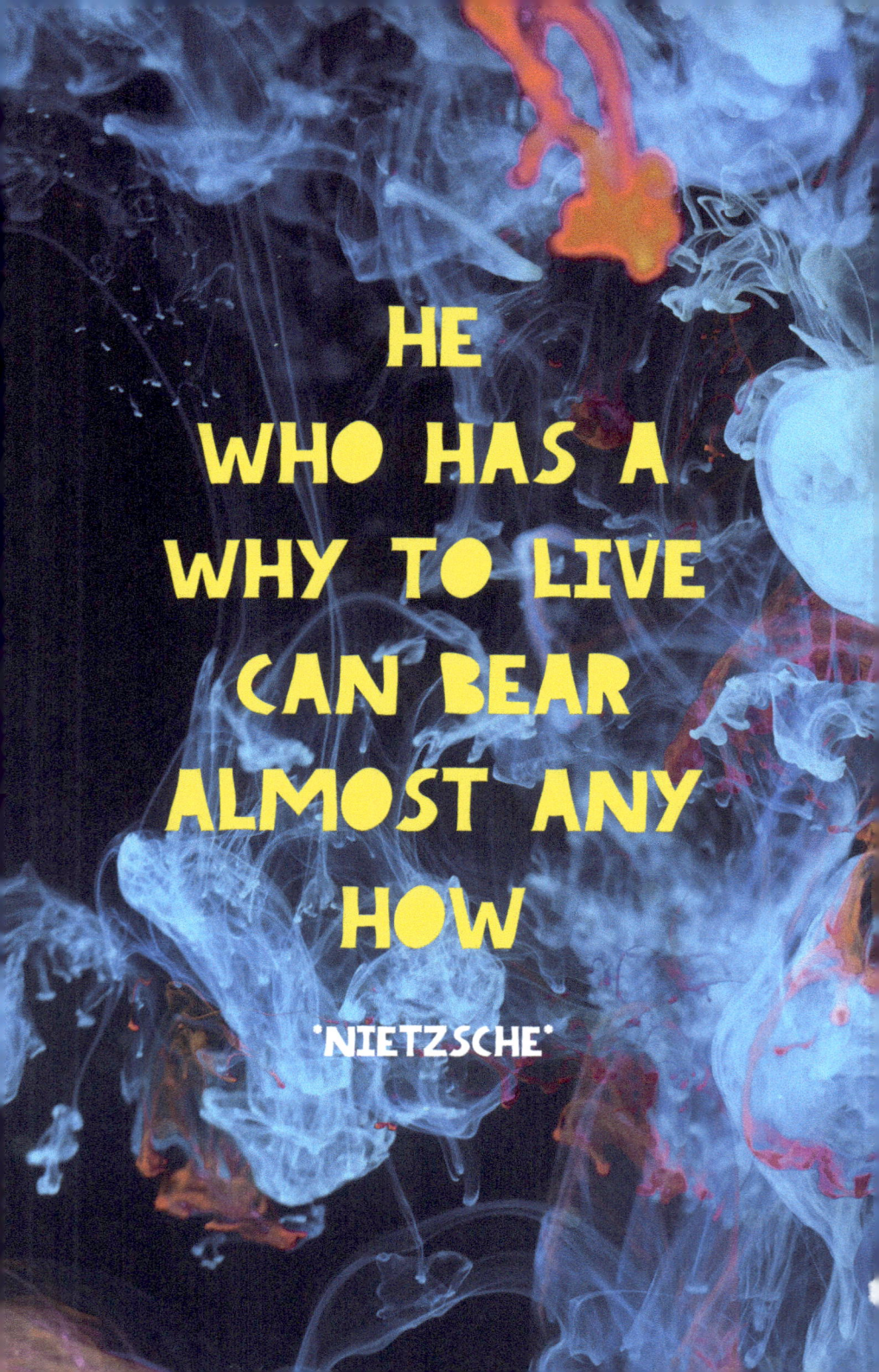

ARE YOU CURRENTLY DOING WHAT MAKES YOU TRULY HAPPY?

WHAT'S STOPPING YOU FROM MAKING THIS ONE THE BEST YEAR OF YOUR LIFE?

THE TWO ENEMIES OF HUMAN HAPPINESS ARE PAIN AND BOREDOM

"SCHOPENHAUER"

WHAT ARE YOU GONNA TAKE LESS SERIOUSLY THIS YEAR?

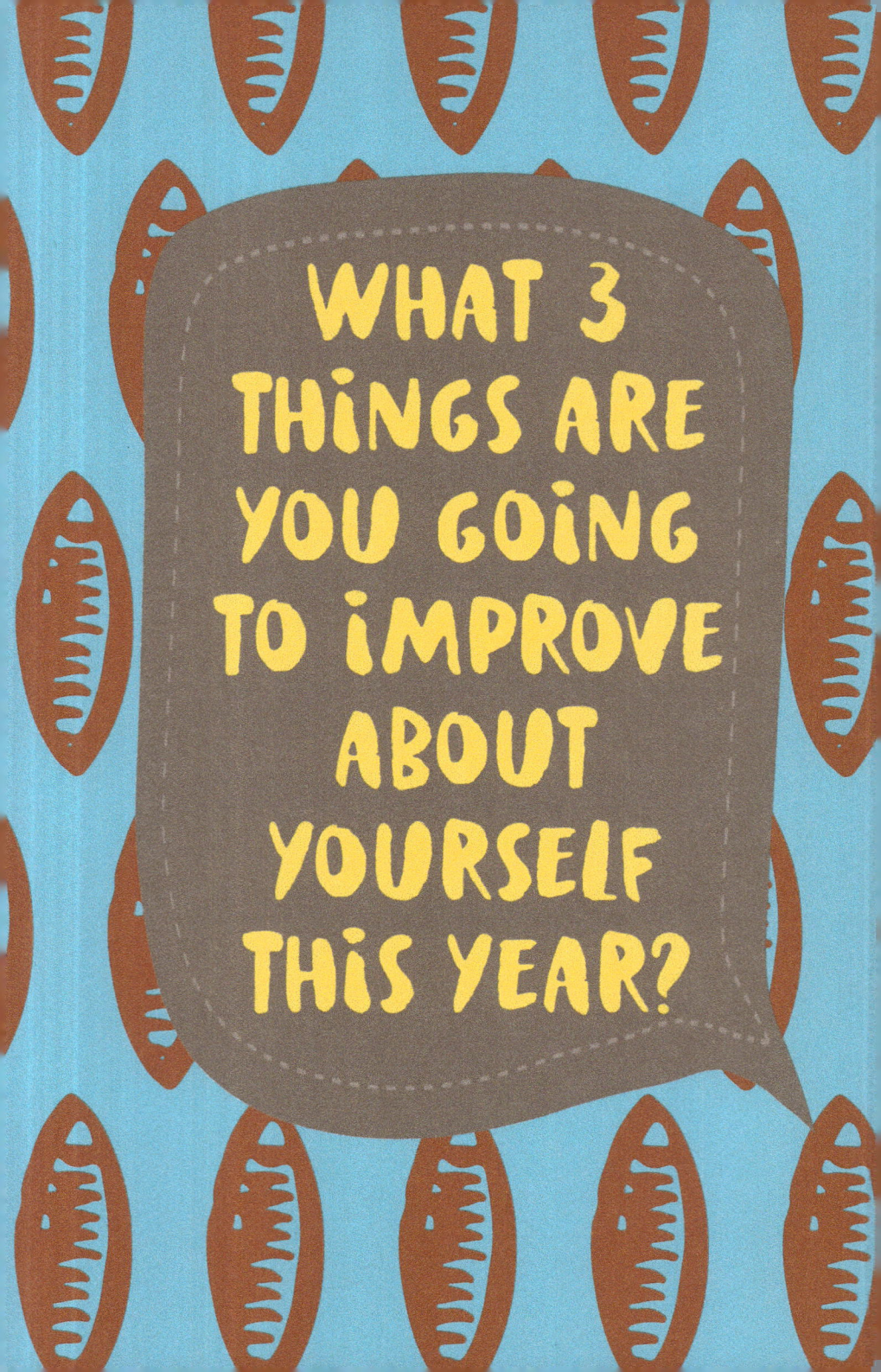

aRe you GoiNG To Be eVeN CooLeR??

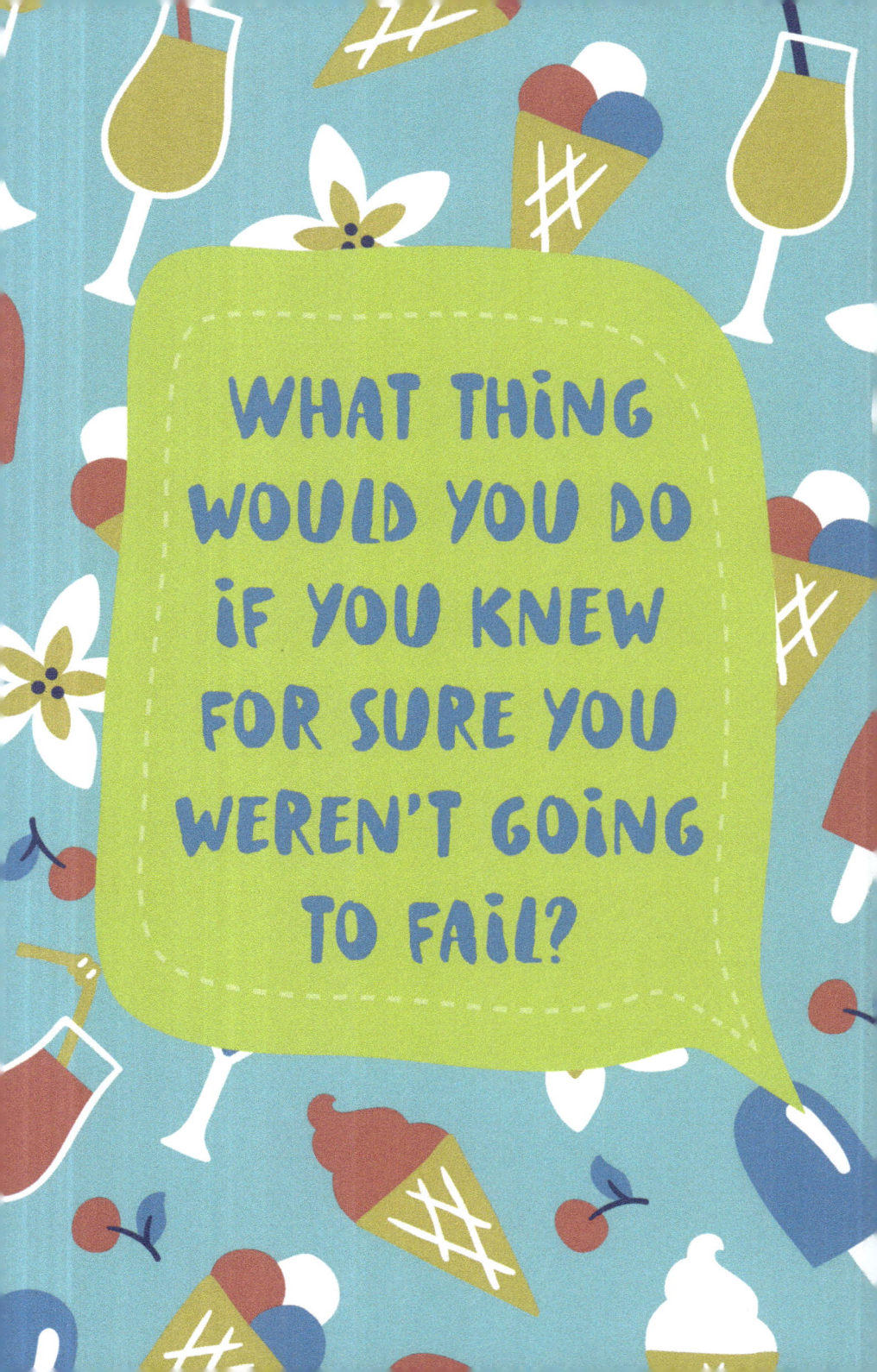

My 3 goals for this year are:

GOALS

aND you'Re GoNNa GeT THeM

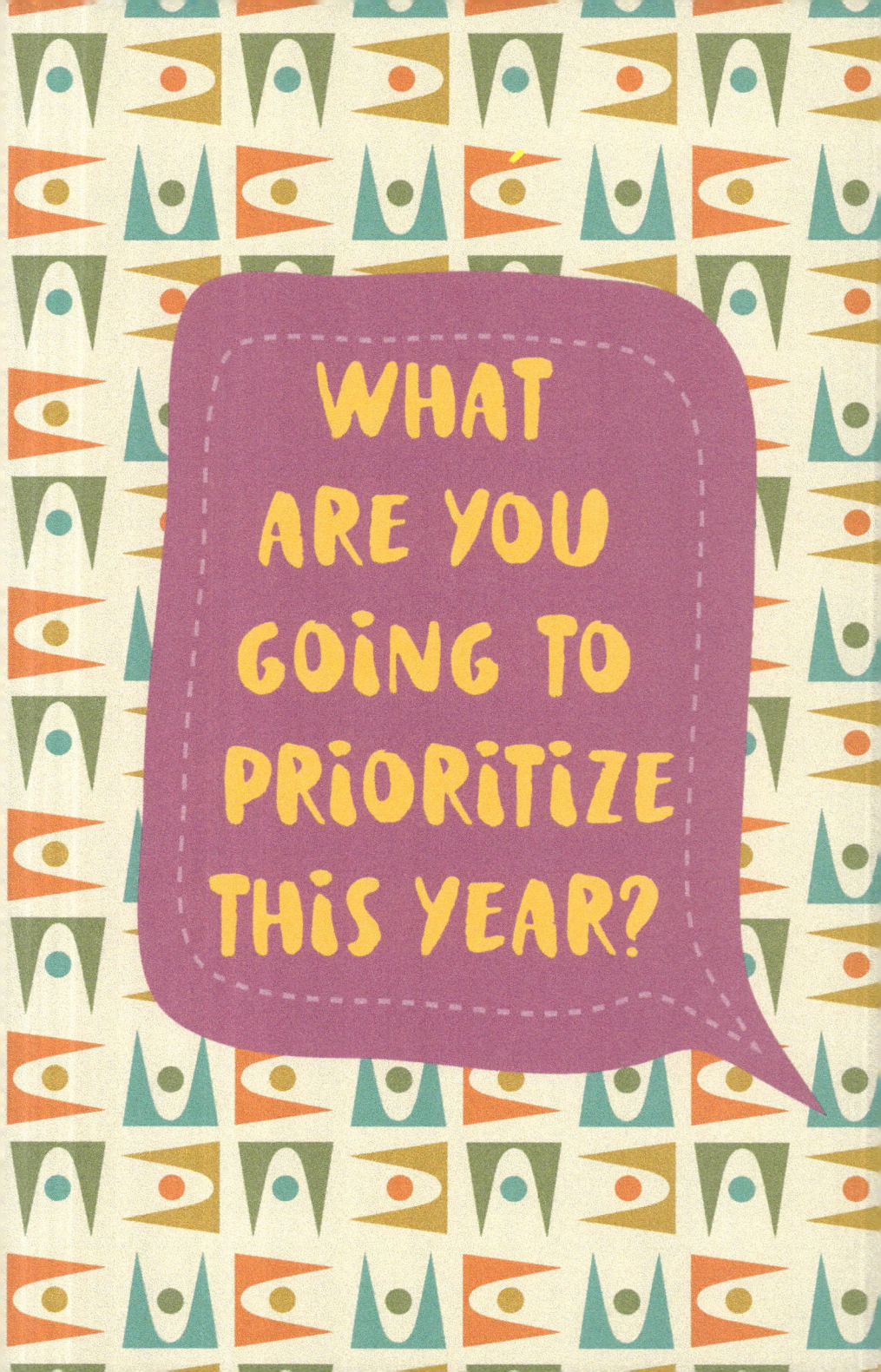

Everyone sees what you appear to be. Few experience what you really are

"MAQUIAVELO"

IN ONE SENTENCE: WHO YOU ARE?

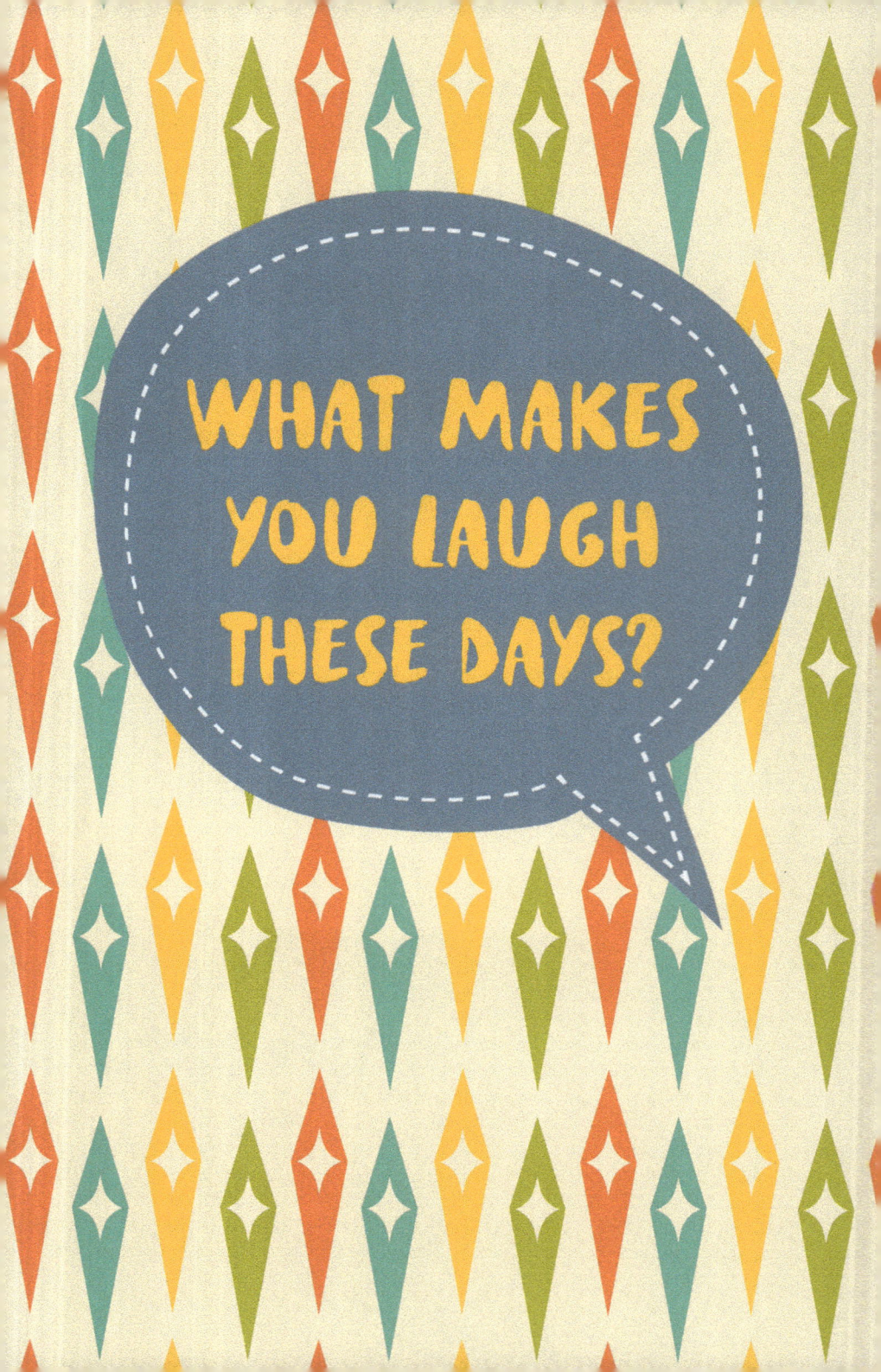

WRITE WITH BIG LETTERS «I'M AMAZING»

(yes, you are)

> THERE IS NO SUCH THING AS AN EMPTY WORD, ONLY ONE THAT IS WORN OUT YET REMAINS FULL.
>
> 'HEIDEGGER'

WHAT'S THE BIGGEST CHALLENGE YOU'RE FACING RIGHT NOW?

WHAT PLACE DO YOU ~~WANT~~ GOING TO VISIT THIS YEAR?

NO VACANCY

MOTEL

POOL

HAPPY BiRTHDAY!!

www.ingramcontent.com/pod-product-compliance
Lightning Source LLC
LaVergne TN
LVHW061631070526
838199LV00071B/6649